Mandala Colouring page

DreamyECO

✳ Tag your beautiful creation
at #dreamyecomandalas

📷 Lets connect @dreamyeco

📓 Browse our other journal designs:
bit.ly/journals_dreamyeco

🔗 See our other works at: bit.ly/dreamyeco_links

Made in United States
Orlando, FL
03 December 2021

11119366R00083